World Traveler

Travel to Russia

Christine Layton

Lerner Publications ◆ Minneapolis

For Art and Elaine

Content consultant: Mikhail Blinnikov, Professor of Geography at Saint Cloud State University, Saint Cloud, MN

Lerner Publications Company
An imprint of Lerner Publishing Group, Inc.
241 First Avenue North
Minneapolis, MN 55401 USA

For reading levels and more information, look up this title at www.lernerbooks.com.

Main body text set in Adrianna Regular.
Typeface provided by Chank.

Library of Congress Cataloging-in-Publication Data

Names: Layton, Christine Marie, 1985– author.
Title: Travel to Russia / Christine Layton.
Description: Minneapolis : Lerner Publications, [2022] | Series: Searchlight books - world traveler | Includes bibliographical references and index. | Audience: Ages 8–11 | Audience: Grades 4–6 | Summary: "As the largest country in the world, Russia boasts rich and varied cultures and landscapes. Check out beautiful countrysides and the bold architecture of Russia's cities in this examination of Russia's vast and exciting history"— Provided by publisher.
Identifiers: LCCN 2021026359 (print) | LCCN 2021026360 (ebook) | ISBN 9781728441702 (lib. bdg.) | ISBN 9781728448879 (pbk.) | ISBN 9781728445045 (eb pdf)
Subjects: LCSH: Russia (Federation)—Juvenile literature.
Classification: LCC DK510.23 .L39 2022 (print) | LCC DK510.23 (ebook) | DDC 914.704—dc23

LC record available at https://lccn.loc.gov/2021026359
LC ebook record available at https://lccn.loc.gov/2021026360

Manufactured in the United States of America
1-49925-49768-9/14/2021

Table of Contents

Chapter 1

GEOGRAPHY AND CLIMATE

From the window of your train, you see rolling plains and low hills. You cross the Ural Mountains going east. The huge taiga forests and steppes of Siberia pass by. You turn south into hills and see more mountains. They hide Siberian tigers, Amur leopards, and Kamchatka brown bears. You are traveling across the world's largest country, Russia.

Siberian tiger

Land

Russia stretches across Europe and Asia. It borders the Arctic Ocean and the Pacific Ocean. Russia is neighbors with fourteen countries including China, Finland, and Mongolia.

The land holds many natural resources such as oil, minerals, and natural gas. Developers use roads and gas pipelines to reach them. But the landscape can be harsh. Wild forest covers almost half of Russia. There are also deserts, mountains, and tundra.

Landforms

Plains cover much of Russia, but so do mountains. The Ural Mountains stretch across Russia. The Caucasus mountain range is in the south. It is home to Mount Elbrus, the highest mountain in Europe.

Many people hike in the Ural Mountains.

THE AKTRU RIVER

▼

Huge lakes and rivers run across the country. They freeze and thaw with the seasons. Russia's Volga River is the longest river in Europe. Lake Baikal is the deepest lake in the world.

The Chara Sands is a desert in eastern Russia. It has dunes and sandstorms. Forest, rivers, and swamps surround the desert.

Some of the volcanoes in the Kamchatka Peninsula are still active.

The Kamchatka Peninsula is the land of fire and ice. It stretches north to the frozen Arctic. The peninsula's Ring of Fire is a belt of more than a hundred volcanoes.

Climate

The climate varies across Russia. Some areas are subtropical. Other are subarctic. Even summers are cold in the north. But in the southern steppes, summers are hot and winters are mild. Sochi, in Southern Russia, is one of the few places in Russia with a subtropical climate.

Hills in the steppes of Khakassia, Russia

Most Russians live in cities, but some make their homes in less populated areas.

Homes

Russia is the largest country in the world at 6.6 million square miles (17 million sq. km). But it is not the most populated. There are only about twenty-two people for each square mile (eight per sq. km).

About 75 percent of people live in apartments in western cities. More than twelve million people live in the capital city, Moscow. Five million people live in Saint Petersburg.

There are cities in the Asian part of Russia too. Novosibirsk and Krasnoyarsk are two of the largest. They each have more than a million residents. Vladivostok is a city on the Pacific coast. It takes seven days to travel by train from Moscow to Vladivostok.

Must-See Stop:
Lake Baikal

Lake Baikal is a crescent-shaped lake in Siberia. It is the deepest lake in the world at 4,921 feet (1,500 m) deep. At twenty-five million years old, it's the oldest lake in the world. And it's cold. The ice freezes 6.5 feet (2 m) thick in the winter.

There are types of plants and animals in Lake Baikal that don't live anywhere else. Tourists come to see Baikal seals. They are the only seal that lives in fresh water.

Chapter 2

HISTORY AND GOVERNMENT

Many different peoples have lived in Russia for a very long time. Artifacts tell their history. Native peoples, travelers, and traders mingled together. They came from areas including other parts of Europe, the Middle East, and China. The territory of Russia, once known as Rus, has always been huge.

Early Russia

Vladimir the Great ruled from 980–1015 CE. He converted Russia's people to Orthodox Christianity. The Mongols invaded in 1237. They ruled for over two hundred years. Ivan the Great took control from the Mongols. Around then, Rus became known as Russia.

Ivan the Terrible was the first czar of Russia. He fought for more land. Russia went through years of civil war and invasions after his death. Eventually, Michael Romanov became czar. He was only sixteen. But he brought peace.

Statue of Prince Vladimir the Great

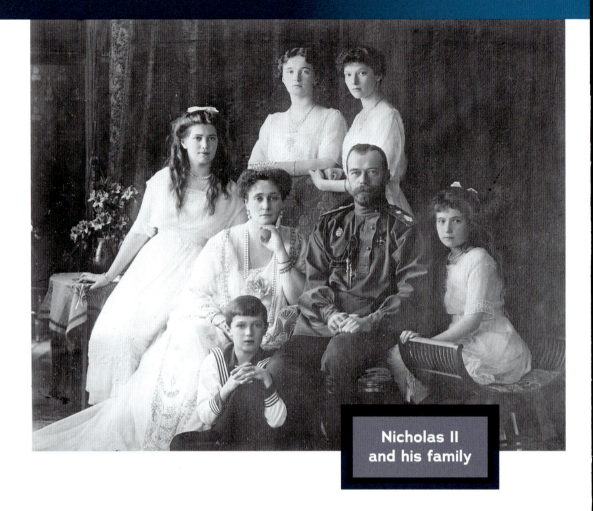

Nicholas II and his family

The End of Czars

The Romanov family ruled Russia for three hundred years. But things began to change. Wars took many lives and resources. People worked hard to make ends meet. In 1917, a revolution ended the Romanov dynasty. Nicholas II was the last czar of Russia.

A new government, the Bolsheviks, took over. Russia's name changed to the Soviet Union. The Soviet Union was a group of fifteen republics.

In 1985, Mikhail Gorbachev led the Communist Party. He made changes to the way the Soviet Union worked with the rest of the world. He wanted the Soviet Union to be more open. For example, he worked with the president of the United States, a past rival. However, in 1991 the Communist government collapsed and the Soviet Union ended.

Former US president Ronald Reagan (*left*) and Mikhail Gorbachev

Government

Today, Russia's full name is the Russian Federation. Russia is a democratic federal republic. Like the United States, it is made up of many smaller regions. Russia has eighty-five territories.

The leader of Russia is the president. Russian citizens elect the president in a national vote. The president chooses government leaders and judges, and controls the armed forces.

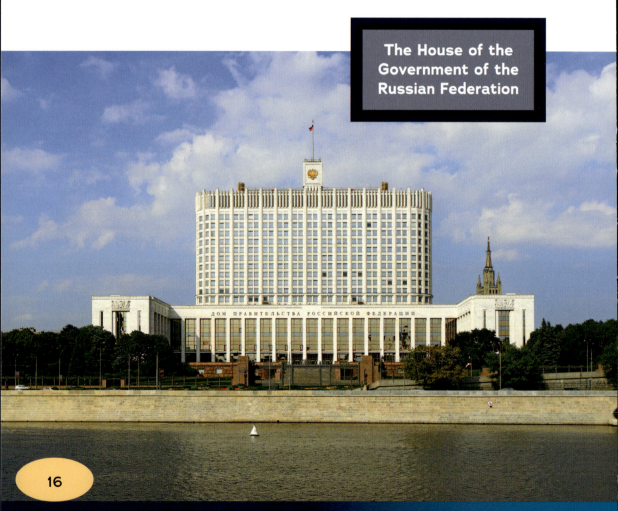

The House of the Government of the Russian Federation

Let's Celebrate:
Russia Day

Russia Day is a national holiday. On June 12, the start of the Russian Federation is celebrated. The president holds a ceremony at the Kremlin. Many people attend it. There, Russians earn awards for writing, science, and work that helped others. People attend concerts and fireworks. Schools and offices close for the celebration.

Chapter 3

CULTURE AND PEOPLE

Most Russians are part of an ethnic group called Slavs. But Russia has a large variety of people. There are almost two hundred ethnic groups in Russia. They include Ukrainians, Bashkirs, and Tatars. Each ethnic group has its own customs, religion, and language. Yet many Russian citizens have some things in common.

Food and Art

Some dishes are popular across Russia. Borscht is a soup made of meat stock, beets, and other vegetables. It has a sweet-and-sour flavor. Another favorite, blini, are round, thin pancakes. Blini are often topped with sour cream, honey, or jam.

BEETS GIVE BORSCHT ITS BRIGHT RED COLOR.

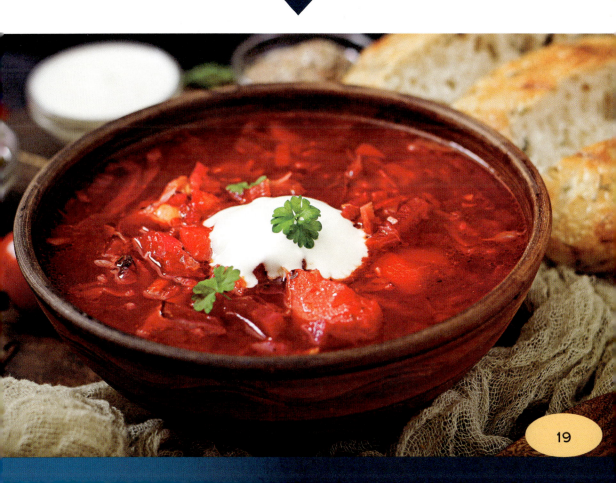

Russian ballet is popular. It is famous around the world. The Russian Ballet tours the world with productions like *The Sleeping Beauty*, *The Nutcracker*, and *Swan Lake*.

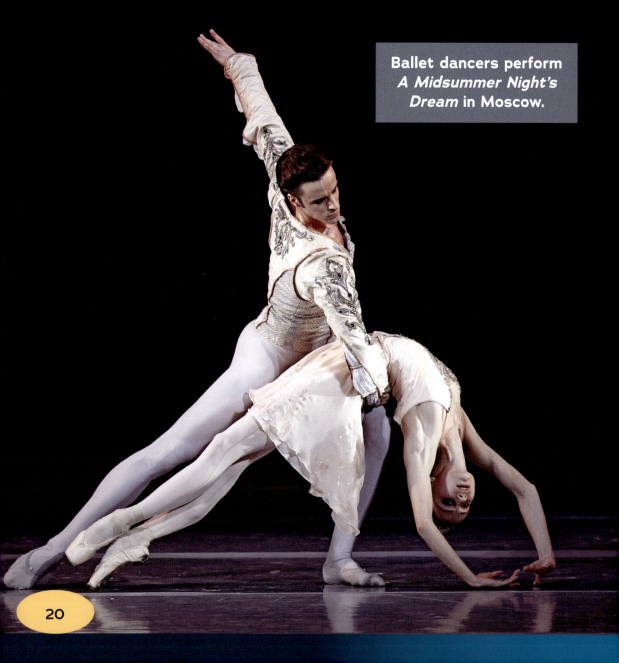

Ballet dancers perform *A Midsummer Night's Dream* in Moscow.

Saint Basil's Cathedral on Red Square in Moscow

Religion

Russia has many religions. About 20 percent of Russian people practice Orthodox Christianity. Moscow alone has over one thousand churches and cathedrals. Saint Basil's Cathedral is the most famous Orthodox Christian church in Russia. About 10 percent of the population is Muslim and practices Islam. The Moscow Cathedral Mosque is one of the biggest mosques in Russia. It is recognizable for its gold domed roof. Other Russians practice Judaism or Buddhism. People also learn about the older traditions of their ancestors.

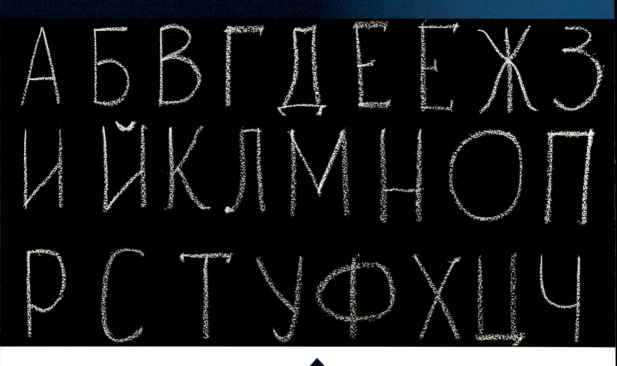

PART OF THE CYRILLIC ALPHABET

Language and Writing

Russian is the official language of Russia. But more than one hundred languages are spoken in Russia. Many people speak more than one language. They learn Russian and a local language.

The Russian language has used the Cyrillic alphabet since the Middle Ages. The Cyrillic alphabet is based on the Greek alphabet. Peter the Great made the Cyrillic alphabet easier to read. In 1918, the government removed some letters from the alphabet. This made the alphabet even easier to use and read.

Let's Celebrate:
Russian Winter Festival

Russia has a winter holiday break starting on New Year's Day, January 1, and ending on Russian Christmas, January 7. People perform traditional Russian songs and dances. They play games, make crafts, and eat special foods.

Russian winter traditions include the myth of Ded Moroz, or Grandfather Frost. He has a white beard and wears a warm coat and heavy boots. Ded Moroz travels with Snegurochka, the snow maiden. Together, they deliver gifts on New Year's Eve.

Chapter 4

LIFE IN RUSSIA

Long ago, Vikings and Mongols rode boats and horses across Russia. Today, technology connects the country. The Trans-Siberian Railroad connects the continents of Europe and Asia. It is one of the longest railroads in the world. About 80 percent of Russian people have internet access at home. It helps people stay connected.

Russia also looks to the stars. The Soviet Union sent the first satellite to space in 1957 and the first person in 1961. Russia participates in International Space Station projects.

Plans for the future

Russian leaders want to manufacture more technology. They hope to sell these tools to the rest of the world. Russian leaders also plan to build a new space station in 2025.

The Soyuz MS-18 rocket launches, carrying Russian astronauts into outer space in April 2021.

But manufacturing and mining bring air pollution. Logging takes away animal homes and causes soil to wash away. Large cities face pollution problems. The Russian government aims to fix these problems. Government officials hope to focus on trade instead of mining. They want to save Russia's natural resources.

The city of Moscow

Russia is united by pride. Its traditions and history bring people together. The country has gone through many changes over the centuries. Russians have worked hard during these changes. They remember their long and eventful past and look forward to an exciting future.

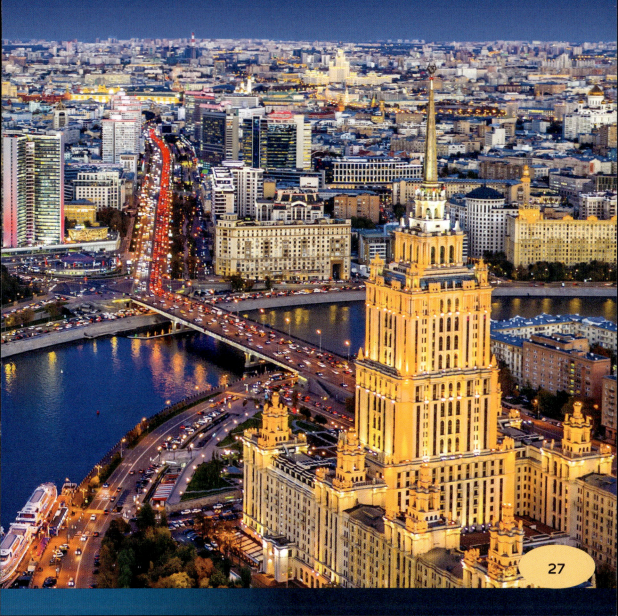

Must-See Stop:
Moscow

Moscow sits on the Moskva River. The Red Square lies at the heart of Moscow. The Red Square is a beloved cultural landmark. It is surrounded by historic buildings.

From the Red Square, you can see the colorful onion-shaped domes of Saint Basil's Cathedral. You can also see the Moscow Kremlin, a huge fortress. The Kremlin was the center of power for the rulers of the Soviet Union. Now it is the home of the president and a major museum.

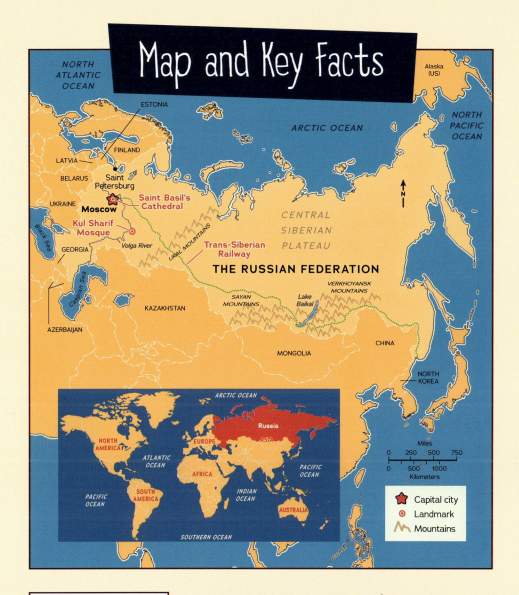

Map and Key Facts

NORTH ATLANTIC OCEAN

Alaska (US)

NORTH PACIFIC OCEAN

ARCTIC OCEAN

ESTONIA

FINLAND

LATVIA

BELARUS

Saint Petersburg

UKRAINE

Moscow

Saint Basil's Cathedral

Kul Sharif Mosque

Volga River

GEORGIA

Black Sea

Caspian Sea

AZERBAIJAN

URAL MOUNTAINS

Trans-Siberian Railway

CENTRAL SIBERIAN PLATEAU

THE RUSSIAN FEDERATION

VERKHOYANSK MOUNTAINS

SAYAN MOUNTAINS

Lake Baikal

KAZAKHSTAN

MONGOLIA

CHINA

NORTH KOREA

ARCTIC OCEAN

Russia

NORTH AMERICA

EUROPE

ASIA

ATLANTIC OCEAN

AFRICA

PACIFIC OCEAN

PACIFIC OCEAN

SOUTH AMERICA

INDIAN OCEAN

AUSTRALIA

SOUTHERN OCEAN

Miles
0   250   500   750
0   500   1000
Kilometers

⭐ Capital city
◉ Landmark
⋀⋀ Mountains

Flag of Russia

- **Continents: Asia and Europe**
- **Capital city: Moscow**
- **Population: 142,320,790**
- **Languages: Russian is the official language with over one hundred other languages also spoken**

Glossary

ballet: a form of dance that tells a story through movement, music, costumes, and scenery

czar: an emperor of Russia before the revolution of 1917

ethnic group: a group of people sharing the same country of origin, language, or culture

manufacture: to make something, often with machines

republic: a form of government where people are ruled by representatives they select

steppe: a wide plain without trees found in southeastern Europe and Asia

subarctic: relating to the area immediately south of the Arctic Circle.

trade: the business of buying and selling goods

tundra: a very cold area where there are no trees and the ground is always frozen

Learn More

Blevins, Wiley. *Russia*. New York: Scholastic, 2018.

Britannica Kids: Russia
  https://kids.britannica.com/kids/article/Russia/345773

Burton, Jesse. *Russia*. New York: Simon Spotlight, 2018.

Hopkinson, Deborah. *Where Is the Kremlin?* New York: Penguin Workshop, 2019.

Kids World Travel Guide: Russia
  https://www.kids-world-travel-guide.com/russia-facts.html

National Geographic Kids: Russia
  https://kids.nationalgeographic.com/geography/countries/article/russia

Index

Photo Acknowledgments

IImage credits: Karel Bartik/Shutterstock.com, p. 5; Aleksandr Zykov/flickr (CC BY-SA 2.0), p. 6; Riska Parakeet/Shutterstock.com, p. 7; Vershinin-M/iStock/Getty Images, p. 8; Alexander Nikitin/Moment/Getty Images, p. 9; Olga_Kovalova/Shutterstock.com, p. 10; Sergey Pesterev/ Wikimedia Commons (CC BY-SA 4.0), p. 11; Vladimir Zhupanenko/Shutterstock.com, p. 13; Library of Congress (LC-DIG-ggbain-14545), p. 14; National Archives/Wikimedia Commons, p. 15; Ludvig14/Wikimedia Commons (CC BY-SA 4.0), p. 16; Skadr/iStock/Getty Images, pp. 17, 28; Timolina/Shutterstock.com, p. 19; Sergey Petrov/Shutterstock.com, p. 20; yulenochekk/ iStock/Getty Images, p. 21; Prostock-studio/Shutterstock.com, p. 22; dimbar76/Shutterstock .com, p. 23; NASA/Bill Ingalls, p. 25; Avigator Fortuner/Shutterstock.com, pp. 26–27; Laura K. Westlund, p. 29.

Cover: Mordolff/E+/Getty Images.